Gu
D
Pub

Steve Davison

COUNTRYSIDE BOOKS
NEWBURY BERKSHIRE

First published 2022
© 2022 Steve Davison

COUNTRYSIDE BOOKS
3 Catherine Road
Newbury, Berkshire

To view our complete range of books,
please visit us at
www.countrysidebooks.co.uk

ISBN 978 1 84674 413 6

*All materials used in the production of this book
carry FSC certification.*

Cover image by Trevor Yorke
Produced by The Letterworks Ltd., Reading
Typeset by KT Designs, St Helens
Printed by Holywell Press, Oxford

Introduction

Dorset offers a lovely mix of scenery including a rugged coastline overlooking the English Channel, the undulating contours of the flower-rich chalk downs and a patchwork of hedge-lined fields which, when combined with a network of paths, bridleways and quiet lanes make the county a joy to explore on foot.

Wandering through picture-postcard villages is like walking through the pages of a Thomas Hardy novel. Hardy, who was born at Higher Bockhampton in 1840 and later lived at Max Gate in Dorchester, based many of his novels on places and characters he knew within Dorset including Evershot, which was known as 'Evershed' in *Tess of the d'Urbervilles*.

The world-famous Jurassic coastline stretches along Dorset's southern edge and includes the well-photographed chalk stack of Old Harry and the south coast's highest point at Golden Cap with far reaching views to the east and west along the coastline. The Jurassic Coast, which also includes East Devon, was designated as England's only natural World

Heritage Site by UNESCO in 2001 due to its rocks, fossils and landforms. Over millennia coastal erosion has exposed an almost continuous sequence of rock formation spanning 185 million years.

Crowning some of Dorset's hills are the remains of Iron Age hillforts. Constructed over 2000 years ago these defensive structures of concentric ditches and earth embankments offer great views from their commanding positions. The walks in this guide visit a number of hillforts including Eggardon Hill, Hambledon Hill and Maiden Castle; the latter is said to be one of the largest and most complex hillforts in Europe.

Take time to admire the tranquillity to be found in an ancient church, enjoy the atmosphere of a cosy village pub, some of which have been around for over 400 years, or just enjoy the abundance of wildlife to be found whilst walking in Dorset's beautiful countryside.

Steve Davison

Publisher's Note

We hope that you obtain considerable enjoyment from this book; great care has been taken in its preparation. Although at the time of publication all routes followed public rights of way or permitted paths, diversion orders can be made and permissions withdrawn.

We cannot, of course, be held responsible for such diversion orders or any inaccuracies in the text which result from these or any other changes to the routes, nor any damage which might result from walkers trespassing on private property. We are anxious, though, that all the details covering the walks are kept up to date, and would therefore welcome information from readers which would be relevant to future editions.

The simple sketch maps that accompany the walks in this book are based on notes made by the author whilst surveying the routes on the ground. They are designed to show you how to reach the start and to point out the main features of the overall circuit, and they contain a progression of numbers that relate to the paragraphs of the text.

However, for the benefit of a proper map, we do recommend that you purchase the relevant Ordnance Survey sheet covering your walk. Ordnance Survey maps are widely available, especially through booksellers and local newsagents.

1 Seatown & Golden Cap

4¾ miles / 7.5km

WALK HIGHLIGHTS

From Langdon Hill the walk meanders past the ruins of the 13th-century St Gabriel's Chapel before heading steeply up to the top of Golden Cap. Named after the colour of the rock, this lofty position – the highest point on the south coast of England at 191m – offers a stunning view including west towards Devon and east to Portland. The route then follows the South West Coast Path for a while down to Seatown and the wonderfully-sited Anchor Inn, before heading back to the start.

THE PUB

The Anchor Inn, Seatown, DT6 6JU.
☎ 01297 489215 www.theanchorinnseatown.co.uk

THE WALK

From the top of the car park turn right along the track for 450m, following it as it curves left round **Langdon Hill**. At a signpost, fork right down a path (**Langdon Woods Walk**) and at the next junction

Guide to Dorset Pub Walks

HOW TO GET THERE AND PARKING: Langdon Hill National Trust car park; head west on A35 from Chideock for ¾ mile and turn left, then left again. **Sat Nav:** DT6 6SF.

MAP: OS Explorer 116 Lyme Regis & Bridport. **Grid Ref:** SY412930.

TERRAIN: Hilly route, gates and stiles, can be muddy.

turn right down to a kissing gate (**St Gabriel's ¾**). Follow the left-hand field edge downhill. Go through field gates either side of a track, with **Filcombe Farm** to the left and continue down the left-hand edge through fields to the bottom. Follow the track through the field gate and immediately fork left (**St Gabriel's ½**) through the trees. Keep ahead on a narrow path beside a stream, cross a footbridge and go through a small gate. Follow the track ahead through fields separated by a gate.

② Turn left up the concrete track to a seat and three-way signpost opposite the 18th-century thatch-roofed **St Gabriel's House**. Keep left up the track, go through a gate and continue up past the ruins of **St Gabriel's Chapel** to enter a field beside a signpost. Fork half-right (signed for **Golden Cap**) up across the field to a kissing gate at the top edge, beside some seats. Continue up the zigzag path, with steps in places, to the trig point on the summit of **Golden Cap**.

③ From the trig point bear left, following the coast path as it zigzags down steps. Go through a kissing gate and turn right to continue down the coast path. Go through a kissing gate (signed **Seatown 1**) heading steeply downhill. Keep ahead through fields separated by a kissing gate to reach a path junction. Go through the kissing gate and keep ahead, soon heading down steps. Continue through two gates 10m apart and follow the path through the trees. Cross a footbridge, go through a kissing gate and continue across the field, then along the enclosed path.

④ Turn right down the lane as it curves left to a junction at the **Golden Cap Holiday Park**. Keep right down to the **Anchor Inn** (right) and the coast ahead (on the left is a car park). Retrace your steps back to the junction and turn right for 15m, then fork right. Follow the concrete track (bridleway) for 350m, passing a couple of cottages, to a junction. Go half-left through a kissing gate signed '**Sea Hill Lane**' and follow the left-hand edge up through two fields separated by a stile. At the top turn left alongside the hedge on your right for 70m, then turn right over a stile beside a gate.

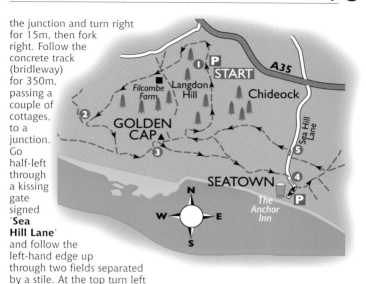

Turn right up the lane for 80m to a track junction and turn left. Follow the hedge-lined track uphill for ¾ mile towards **Langdon Wood**, ignoring all side routes to a junction at the top, with a large and small gate ahead. Turn right through a kissing gate and follow the path up through the trees. Keep right and then bear right along the track for ½ mile skirting round **Langdon Hill** back to the car park.

PLACES OF INTEREST NEARBY

Head to the **Charmouth Heritage Coast Centre** (DT6 6LL) to learn about the geology and fossils of the world-famous Jurassic Coast; then take a walk along the beach looking for fossils.

2 Stoke Abbott

5 miles / 8km

WALK HIGHLIGHTS

The West Dorset town of Beaminster, with its honey-coloured hamstone buildings, is well worth exploring. In The Square is the Robinson Memorial, often referred to as 'Julia', built in memory of Elizabeth Julia Robinson of Parnham. The picturesque village of Stoke Abbott is home to The New Inn, a lovely thatch-roofed 17th-century pub with garden, there is also the Church of St Mary the Virgin with its beautifully carved 11th-century font, whilst from lofty Gerrard's Hill you can enjoy some great views.

THE PUB

The New Inn, Stoke Abbott, DT8 3JW.
☎ 01308 868333   www.newinnstokeabbott.co.uk

THE WALK

❶ From the memorial in **The Square**, with the A3066 behind you, head south-west down **Church Street** to a junction. Turn left along **St Mary Well Street**, later keeping right up along the cul-de-sac past houses. Continue along the track, where this goes left at a cattle grid (private),

8

HOW TO GET THERE AND PARKING: The Square in Beaminster; 6 miles north of Bridport on the A3066; pay and display parking or on-street parking nearby. **Sat Nav:** DT8 3AS.

MAP: OS Explorer 116 Lyme Regis & Bridport. **Grid Ref:** ST480013.

TERRAIN: Some steep bits, gates and stiles, can be muddy.

keep right through a gate. Follow the left field edge and leave through a gate. Continue across the next field, go through a gate and follow the enclosed route. Pass a gate, and after 350m look for a kissing gate on the right, go through this and head up across the field to a kissing gate.

Cross over the track, through a small gate and keep ahead through the field down to a small gate. Continue to a path junction. Do not cross the footbridge ahead, but turn right (**Jubilee Trail**). Cross the next footbridge, go through a small gate and head up through the field, passing a tree. At the top edge turn left, go through a gate and follow a hedge-lined track (**Long Barrow Lane**) for ½ mile.

Turn left along the minor road, passing the **Horsehill Farm** turning, to a junction on the right in **Stoke Abbott**. The onward route turns right here, but before that keep ahead for 150m to **The New Inn** on the left. For the church continue along the road as it bends left to a junction, keep ahead for 30m and turn left to the church; retrace your steps.

From the pub head back to the junction and turn left up the drive for 400m, signed 'bridleway – private road to **Chart Knolle** and **Chart Vale**'. At a signpost, 25m after some gateposts, turn left up through the trees. Go through a small gate, continue with a house over to the right and go through another gate to a signed four-way junction. Turn right through a small gate ('**Beaminster 1**') and follow the right-hand fence (house on right); now following the **Wessex Ridgeway**. Cross two stiles, go through a gate and keep ahead alongside the left-hand fence up to **Gerrard's Hill**.

Head east downhill, cross stiles either side of a track and continue

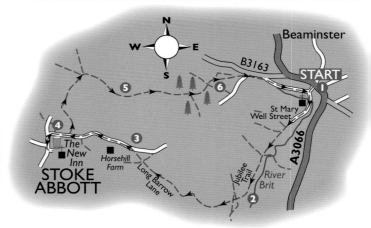

through the field. Cross a stile on the left beside a tree and head steeply downhill, crossing another stile. Go straight over a track, then through a small gate and over a footbridge. Keep ahead through the wood (**Woodland Trust**). Go through a small gate and bear right then left along the track. After the last building, turn right to a signed path junction and go through the gate.

6 Head diagonally left down across the field and leave via a stile in the corner. Keep ahead along the track and turn right along the lane to a T-junction. Go left for 20m, then right through a small gate and follow the signed path through the meadow to a small gate. Continue along the track and then along **Shorts Lane** to a junction. Keep ahead along **Church Street** passing **St Mary's Church** and turn left at the next junction back to **The Square**.

PLACES OF INTEREST NEARBY

Visit **Mapperton House and Gardens**, home of the Earl and Countess of Sandwich and voted the "nation's finest manor house" (DT8 3NR; www.mapperton.com).

3 Askerswell

6¼ miles / 10km

WALK HIGHLIGHTS

Just to the north of Askerswell lies Eggardon Hill which is crowned by the impressive earthworks of an Iron Age hillfort that give a great view. In the 18th century a local smuggler, Isaac Gulliver, took advantage of the hill's commanding position and created a small octagonal plantation of trees (no longer there) to act as a landmark for his ships and help guide them to the coast. Tucked below the hill is the Spyway Inn, with its lovely large garden overlooking rolling fields, which dates back to 1845.

THE PUB

The Spyway Inn, Askerswell, DT2 9EP.
☎ 01308 485250 www.thespywayinn.com

THE WALK

From the crossroads, with the trig point 100m to the left, follow the lane towards **Powerstock** and **West Milton** for ¾ mile, with views to the right, later heading downhill. As the lane bends right, fork left (straight on) along a track for almost 1 mile as it descends and later curves left before passing **Marsh Farm** to a three-way junction.

Guide to Dorset Pub Walks

HOW TO GET THERE AND PARKING: Spyway Road and King's Lane crossroads; from the A35 between Bridport and Dorchester follow the road signposted towards Askerswell. Keep left to a cross-junction and follow signs for Spyway to a T-junction and turn right up to the crossroads after passing a trig point; limited roadside parking to the right. **Sat Nav:** DT2 0DS.

MAP: OS Explorer 117 Cerne Abbas & Bere Regis. **Grid Ref:** SY547945.

TERRAIN: Some steep bits, gates and stiles, can be muddy.

2 Turn right along the lane for ¼ mile, later heading up past the abutments of an old railway bridge (the house on the right was once the railway station). At the brow of the hill turn left over a stile in the hedge and head across the field. Cross a stile and bear half-left down through the trees to a four-way track junction and keep ahead; the track going left to right was once the branch line between Bridport and Maiden Newton which operated between 1857 and 1975.

3 Follow the track (footpath) gently uphill, soon with wooded **Knowle Hill** on your left. At the end of the wood keep ahead down through the field staying close to the left-hand edge. Continue through the next field passing to the right of a barn at **Lodersland Farm**. Keep ahead and soon bear right along the track as it crosses a stream and curves left uphill, passing under the overhead power lines. Follow the track as it swings hard right and continues to join a minor road. Turn left up past **The Spyway Inn** (right) to a cross-junction.

4 Turn left along the drive (private road - bridleway only) towards **South Eggardon House and Farm** for just under ½ mile. Some 150m after passing a house on your right, as the drive nears **Eggardon House**, go right through a field gate. Follow the track as it bears half-left and heads towards another gate. Do not go through the gate (private), but turn right up alongside the fence on your left. Turn left through a small gate and follow the bridleway for ½ mile along the bottom of a steep slope beside a line of trees at first and then later heading up to the top corner.

5 Go through the gate and turn left up the lane for 350m. Just after the

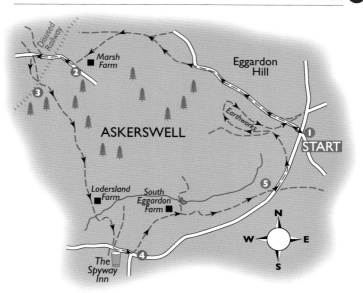

scrub and bushes on the left, turn left through a gate and follow the enclosed bridleway as it swings right. On reaching a signed four-way junction, go through the left-hand gate and head clockwise along the top of the earthworks on **Eggardon Hill** (National Trust) enjoying the views. Turn right following the fence and leave through the gate used earlier. Then go through the second gate on the left, following the bridleway across the field to a gate. Turn right along the lane back to the crossroads.

PLACES OF INTEREST NEARBY

Head to the busy market town of **Bridport** and take a tour round **Palmers Brewery** (DT6 4JA: www.palmersbrewery.com) who have been brewing in Dorset since 1794. A short distance south is **West Bay** with its famous honey-coloured cliffs that form part of the Jurassic Coast.

4 Evershot
4 miles (6.3 km)

WALK HIGHLIGHTS
Exploring Evershot is like stepping into a Thomas Hardy novel. In Hardy's *Tess of the d'Urbervilles*, where Evershot is known as 'Evershed', The Acorn Inn, a 16th-century coaching inn, is known as the 'The Sow & Acorn'. Near the Parish Church of St Osmond, which dates back to the 12th century, is Tess Cottage, where Tess had breakfast in a 'cottage by the church'. The oldest relic in the village is the Evershot Stones, three prehistoric standing stones now forming a seat. Local legend calls them the 'Three Dumb Sisters', who were turned to stone for dancing on the Sabbath.

THE PUB
The Acorn Inn, Evershot, DT2 0JW.
☎ 01935 83228   www.acorn-inn.co.uk

THE WALK
1 From the junction at the small triangular-shaped green with its central

HOW TO GET THERE AND PARKING: The village green in Evershot; 1½ miles west of the A37 between Dorchester and Yeovil; limited roadside parking. **Sat Nav:** DT2 0JY.

MAP: OS Explorer 117 Cerne Abbas & Bere Regis. **Grid Ref:** ST575046.

TERRAIN: Fairly easy walking on tracks, some gates, no stiles.

tree and stone seat – the **Evershot Stones**, head north along **Park Lane** heading away from the main road, passing a 'private road – footpath only' sign. Follow the drive to a Y-junction and take the right-hand fork, signed '**Bridleway Rocks Lane**'. This soon becomes a rough track and continues uphill with a house to your right. At the top of the rise keep ahead, passing a vehicle barrier, then follow the track downhill with trees on the left and a fence on the right.

At the bottom the track splits, take the left-hand fork. Go through a gate and continue through the field with a fence on the right, beyond this you can see **Lucerne Lake** (private) and later the thatched boathouse. Leave through another gate and at the junction, fork right. Follow the bridleway as it swings right into a field and then turns left to follow the left-hand boundary. Go through a gate and continue along the track, passing through another gate to reach a cross-junction with a tarred drive.

Turn left along the drive, crossing the cattle grid and passing **Chetnole Lodge** (house). Continue down the drive and cross two cattle grids either side of a bridge. Keep ahead, following the drive up to a T-junction. Turn left – now following the **Hardy Way** and **Macmillan Way** – following the drive towards **Melbury House** and **St Mary's Chapel** (both private); the house, which has been in the Strangways family since 1500, has a striking hexagonal tower. After passing another cattle grid (with the house ahead) turn right following the drive for 200m to a junction and fork left. Shortly pass a cattle grid to enter the deer park – keep a lookout for the deer. Continue along the drive for 650m heading uphill and leave the deer park at another cattle grid.

Keep ahead along the drive to the large gates and gateposts topped with lions and leave via the steps on the left. Continue along the drive, passing the junction used earlier back to the main street at the common. Turn right and almost immediately turn right again along **Back Lane**. Follow this as it curves left and later curves left again; on the left is **St John's Well**, the source of the River Frome. Continue to a T-junction beside the **Parish Church of St Osmond** (left) and the thatch-roofed **Tess Cottage** (right). Turn left down **Fore Street** through the village passing **The Acorn Inn** (left) and the **Evershot Bakery**, which has been baking since 1857, to arrive back at the start.

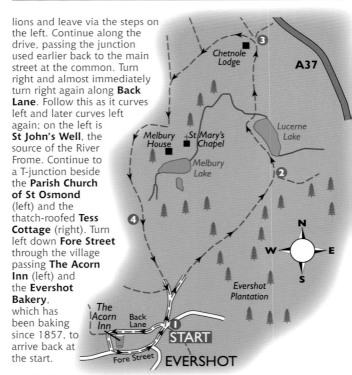

PLACES OF INTEREST NEARBY

Visit **Dorset Wildlife Trust's Kingcombe Centre** at Lower Kingcombe, where there are nature trails, a wildlife garden and a café (DT2 0EQ). Or head to **Yetminster**, a picturesque village of honey-coloured limestone cottages, where local farmer Benjamin Jesty conducted smallpox experiments some 20 years before Edward Jenner; there's a Blue Plaque commemorating him in Church Street just south of St Andrew's Church (DT9 6LG).

5 Abbotsbury

5¼ miles / 8.4km

WALK HIGHLIGHTS

Abbotsbury is well-known for its swannery, established by Benedictine monks who built a monastery here in the 11th century. Unfortunately, much of the abbey was destroyed following the Dissolution of the Monasteries in 1539, although the tithe barn and the 14th-century St Catherine's Chapel have survived; the latter affords a great view over the coast. The walk also follows the former Abbotsbury Railway which operated between 1885 and 1952.

THE PUB

The Swan Inn, Abbotsbury, DT3 4JL.
☎ 01305 871249; no website.

THE WALK

Exit the car park and turn right alongside the B3157 to the **Swan Inn** (right) with its garden overlooking fields. Cross over to continue along the pavement and go left along the track just past **Glebe Close** (left), following the **Hardy Way**. Keep left of the house, soon passing the former railway building (left) and follow the former railway for 1 mile. At the farm, pass a large gate and keep ahead along the track, passing some houses over to your left, to a road (B3157).

17

Guide to Dorset Pub Walks

HOW TO GET THERE AND PARKING: Abbotsbury Car Park; situated on the B3157 between Weymouth and Bridport, pay and display parking off Rodden Row in the village. **Sat Nav:** DT3 4JL.

MAP: OS Explorer OL15 Purbeck & South Dorset. **Grid Ref:** SY578853.

TERRAIN: Hilly walk, gates and stiles, can be muddy.

2 Turn left along the pavement to a junction with **Front Street** in **Portesham**; ahead is the **Kings Arms**. Follow the main road as it curves right to pass **Duck's Farm Shop and Café** before crossing the road to continue along the pavement. Turn right at the entrance to **Portesham Dairy Farm Campsite**.

3 Keep left past a large gate (campsite on your right), still following the **Hardy Way**. Cross a footbridge, go through a small gate and follow the left-hand field edge through two fields separated by a gate. At the far left-hand corner turn left through a gate, then turn right (boundary on your right). Go through a small gate and keep ahead to a path junction at **East Elworth**. Turn right through a fence gap (**Hardy Way** goes left) and follow the drive past the buildings to a lane.

4 Turn right, following the lane as it curves left through **West Elworth**. Where the lane bends right, turn left along the track (bridleway to **Abbotsbury**). Keep to the track as it swings right and continue for 150m. Turn left through a large gate and follow the path up between hedges. Continue over the brow of the hill and through a large gate.

5 Turn right over a stile and follow the **South West Coast Path** through the trees. Go through a small gate and continue along the left-hand boundary through two fields separated by a stile. Cross a stone stile into a third field and continue, ignoring a crossing track. At the footpath sign, go over a stile and continue with the fence on your right. Cross another stile and start descending. At the marker post turn left down to the hedge. Turn right, go left over a stone stile, then right to a stile and down some steps.

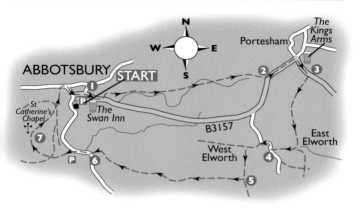

Keep ahead along the lane and fork left along the entrance drive of **Abbotsbury Swannery** (car park on right). Keep to the track as it bears right (swannery entrance on left; www.abbotsbury-tourism. co.uk/swannery) to a footpath sign (straight on heads back to the village). Turn left (permissive path), cross the stile and continue up to the wall. Keep ahead to a marker stone and turn left along the **South West Coast Path** to another marker stone. Turn right, steeply uphill to **St Catherine's Chapel**.

Head diagonally right down the path. Go through a gate and keep ahead along the track to the main street (B3157) in **Abbotsbury**. Turn right and keep right to pass **The Ilchester Arms**. At the next junction go left (**Rodden Row**) and continue back to the car park; the right-hand fork (**Church Street**) leads to **St Nicholas' Church**.

PLACES OF INTEREST NEARBY
Abbotsbury Subtropical Gardens, established in 1765 by Elizabeth, Countess of Ilchester, is filled with exotic plants (DT3 4LA; www.abbotsbury-tourism.co.uk/gardens).

6 Langton Herring

4½ miles / 7.6km

WALK HIGHLIGHTS

Langton Herring, Dorset's only 'Doubly Thankful' village that did not suffer any fatalities during both World Wars, has a number of picturesque thatched cottages and a pub that's been around for almost 400 years. The Fleet Lagoon, an 8-mile-long stretch of water sheltered behind the large shingle barrier of Chesil Beach, is a favoured location for wildfowl – so don't forget your binoculars.

THE PUB

The Elm Tree Inn, Langton Herring, DT3 4HU.
☎ 01305 871257   www.theelmtreeinn.co.uk

THE WALK

1 From the roadside parking area head south up the left-hand verge of the B3157 for 100m to the brow of the hill and the junction for **Buckland Ripers** and **Nottington**. Turn right across the road to a track opposite. Bear left into the field and then follow the bridleway along the right-hand edge through two fields separated by two small gates.

HOW TO GET THERE AND PARKING: Roadside parking area on the B3157, halfway between Portesham and Chickerell, just north of Buckland Ripers junction. **Sat Nav:** DT3 4HH.

MAP: OS Explorer OL15 Purbeck & South Dorset. **Grid Ref:** SY622831.

TERRAIN: Few short climbs, gates and 1 stile, can be muddy.

Leave the second field through the field gate, ignore the crossing path and continue straight on down the track to a field gate.

Turn left along the lane for a 1/3 mile as it curves left, then right and later left again. Head up a slight rise to a junction and turn right, following the lane past cottages to its end at **Ivy Cottage**. Keep ahead to the left of the garage and go through the small gate into a field. Continue along the right-hand fence and where this turns right, keep ahead across the field and then keep to the left side of the hedge. Leave through a gate to a path junction in the next field and keep ahead, staying in the field, following the **South West Coast Path** signposted towards **Ferrybridge**.

Go through a small gate into the next field and continue alongside the right-hand boundary. Go through a kissing gate and turn along the field edge towards the water and a couple of seats. After admiring the views continue along the field edge, keeping the water on your right. Go through kissing gates either side of a track; up to the left is a row of white-washed cottages. Continue along the right-hand field edge, still with the water on your right. Keep ahead through the next field, then cross a footbridge and keep ahead for 20m to a farm track.

Turn left along the track, now following the **Hardy Way**, soon heading uphill with **Under Cross Plantation** on your left. Keep to the track as it levels out; ahead on the skyline you can see the **Hardy Monument**. At the track junction take the narrow footpath straight on between the bushes to a lane in **Langton Herring**. Turn right along the lane as it curves left to a junction and keep ahead; the lane to the left leads to **St Peter's Church**. Continue, with the **Elm Tree Inn** on your left to a T-junction.

5 Turn right, soon passing a house on your left and a gravel driveway that leads to the **Manor House**, then fork left along the walled track (bridleway sign). At the gate, fork left through the trees to a bridleway / footpath junction. Keep left through the gate and follow the footpath up through the small field to a stile in the top left corner. Keep ahead up across the field to a bridleway at the top edge, rejoining the outward route. Turn right, following the field edge on your left back to the B3157. Cross over and turn left back to the parking area.

PLACES OF INTEREST NEARBY

Visit the **Hardy Monument** high above the village of Portesham for a great view. The tower was built in 1844 in memory of Vice-Admiral Sir Thomas Masterman Hardy, Flag Captain of HMS *Victory* at the Battle of Trafalgar (DT2 9HY).

7 Sandford Orcas

2¾ miles / 4.4km

WALK HIGHLIGHTS

Picturesque Sandford Orcas has a lovely collection of honey-coloured hamstone cottages. The early 16th-century Manor House is said to be one of the best examples of a mostly unaltered Tudor manor house. The Church of St Nicholas is worth a visit, inside there is a 13th-century font and several interesting monuments, including a painted alabaster one above the door to Sir William Knoyle. The village pub – The Mitre Inn – which has a large garden, dates back to 1851 and was originally a cider house.

THE PUB

The Mitre Inn, Sandford Orcas, DT9 4RU.
☎ 01963 220271 www.mitreinn.co.uk

THE WALK

Stand with your back to the village hall and turn right up the road for ½ mile through the village, passing **The Mitre Inn** on your right as you go. At the junction in **Higher Sandford**, just after passing a thatched cottage, turn left beside a small postbox in the wall. Follow **Spring Lane** for 25m and bear left through a small gate into the field.

HOW TO GET THERE AND PARKING: Roadside parking beside the village hall in Sandford Orcas; follow the B3148 from Sherborne towards Marston Magna for 2½ miles to a crossroads and turn right (signs for Trent), then turn right at the T-junction to Sandford Orcas and turn right to the village hall on the right. **Sat Nav:** DT9 4RX.

MAP: OS Explorer 129 Yeovil and Sherborne. **Grid Ref:** ST623207.

TERRAIN: Fairly level walk, gates and stiles, can be muddy, some road walking.

2 Follow the right-hand edge to the far-right corner. Go through a gate in the hedge, head across the field and leave through a gate. Turn left along the concrete track for 20m to a Y-junction and take the right-hand track. Keep ahead at a cross-track junction (farm buildings to left) to join a lane with a stone building on your left. Go straight on along the lane for 300m, passing some houses at **Holway**.

3 At the left-hand bend, fork right (straight on) over a stile (**Monarch's Way** and footpath signs) beside the field gate. Continue through the field following the right-hand hedge, passing a solitary oak tree. Dogleg right-left through a field gate and continue through the next field, now following the hedge on your left towards the far-left corner. Cross two stiles and a footbridge in the hedge 10m right of the left-hand corner and continue across the next field. Cross another two stiles in the hedge, go straight on across the field and leave over a stile in the hedge.

4 Turn left along the lane for 200m to a three-way junction at **Stafford's Green**. Turn right for 25m and then turn left on a track past some barns. Where the track turns right go left through a kissing gate and then bear right to cross a footbridge, still following the **Monarch's Way**. Once across, bear left heading south-west through the long field with a hedge over on the right and trees to the left. On nearing the far-side, fork left and cross the stream again via a footbridge in the trees, then bear right to the hedge.

5 Cross two stiles and continue, keeping the lower field edge over to your right. The manor house and church come into view ahead and the

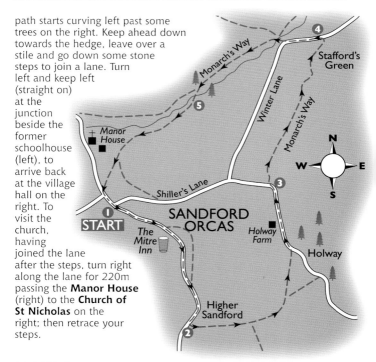

path starts curving left past some trees on the right. Keep ahead down towards the hedge, leave over a stile and go down some stone steps to join a lane. Turn left and keep left (straight on) at the junction beside the former schoolhouse (left), to arrive back at the village hall on the right. To visit the church, having joined the lane after the steps, turn right along the lane for 220m passing the **Manor House** (right) to the **Church of St Nicholas** on the right; then retrace your steps.

PLACES OF INTEREST NEARBY

Visit picturesque **Sherborne**, home to a stunning abbey dating back to Saxon times (DT9 3LQ; www.sherborneabbey.com). The town also has two castles: Sherborne Old Castle, a ruined 12th-century fortified palace (DT9 3SA) and the 16th-century mansion known as Sherborne Castle (DT9 5NR).

8 Martinstown

6 miles / 9.7km

WALK HIGHLIGHTS

Martinstown, aka Winterborne St Martin, is home to The Brewers Arms pub and the 12th-century St Martin's Church. The South Dorset Ridgeway, which is followed briefly, gives great views towards Weymouth and Portland Harbour. The highlight of the walk is Maiden Castle, here you can admire the vast earthworks of one of the largest and most complex Iron Age hillforts in Europe.

THE PUB

The Brewers Arms, Martinstown, DT2 9LB.
☎ 01305 889361   www.thebrewersarms.com

THE WALK

❶ Standing with the church behind you, cross over the B3159 and head south along **Grove Hill** (thatched cottage on right), following the lane up to a right-hand bend. Ignore a footpath to the left and instead fork left (straight on) through a small gate. Follow the bridleway down across the field. Go through a small gate and bear right through the trees.

❷ Keep ahead along the valley with a field on the left and fence on the right. At some trees, bear left along the track to a split and keep left

HOW TO GET THERE AND PARKING: St Martin's Church; from the junction of the A37 and A35 at Dorchester follow the minor road signed to Martinstown and, at the junction with the B3159, turn right along this to the church (limited roadside parking). **Sat Nav:** DT2 9JZ.

MAP: OS Explorer 15 Purbeck & South Dorset. **Grid Ref:** SY647889.

TERRAIN: Hilly route, gates, no stiles, can be muddy, some road walking.

(hedge on the right). Go through a gate and continue up through the field. Leave through another gate and continue, passing to the right of a tumulus (or burial mound) to a junction at the stone wall.

3 Turn left along the **South Dorset Ridgeway** for slightly under ¾ mile to a signed junction, admiring the views on the way. Turn left following the right-hand fence to the far right-hand corner and go through the gate. Head diagonally left across the field, passing some tumuli. Go through a gate into the adjacent field and turn left along the field edge. Once in the next field head diagonally right down across the field to a gate; ahead are views of **Maiden Castle**.

4 Follow the concrete track and drive past buildings and cottages at **Higher Ashton Farm**. With care, cross over the road (B3159) and turn left along it for 65m, then fork right down the lane signposted for **Winterborne Monkton**. Keep ahead at the crossroads and where the lane curves right, go straight on through a small gate. Follow the bridleway up the coombe (valley) to a field gate and follow the enclosed route for 175m to a small gate on the right. Turn right through this to explore the earthworks of **Maiden Castle**; retrace your steps through the gate and turn right.

5 Continue down the enclosed route for 75m to a junction and turn left, following the bridleway as it quickly swings right down to a cross-junction. Turn left, go through a gate and keep ahead towards **Clandon Farm**. Follow the tarred track to the left and right, then right and left, to pass some barns and farm buildings. Keep ahead along the track to a three-way road junction.

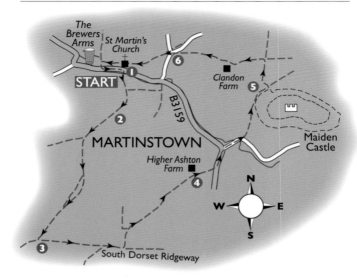

6 Cross over slightly to the right (almost straight on) and go through a small gate just right of a line of trees. Follow the bridleway along the left-hand boundary through two fields separated by a small gate and leave the second field through another small gate. Turn right along the lane for 10m and then turn left through a small gate. Follow the enclosed footpath, passing the church (left). Keep ahead across the estate road to the end of the path. Turn left along the track and then left again, soon passing the **Sheep Washing Pool** (left) to the road (B3159), with **The Brewers Arms** on your right. Turn left alongside the road back to the start.

PLACES OF INTEREST NEARBY

Visit **Dorchester**, established by the Romans and used by Thomas Hardy in *The Mayor of Casterbridge*. Visit Max Gate (DT1 2FN) Thomas Hardy's former home, or the thatched cottage where he was born in 1840 at **Higher Bockhampton** (DT2 8QJ).

9 Cerne Abbas

2¾ miles / 4.4km

WALK HIGHLIGHTS

The Cerne Abbas Giant, a rather large, naked male figure carved into the chalk hillside, is now believed to be over a thousand years old, and just so that you know, the best view is from the air. The village was home to a Benedictine Abbey founded in AD 987, however, all that remains today is the 15th-century Guest House and 16th-century Abbot's Porch; the South Gatehouse was converted to form Abbey House. At the start of the walk, the thatch-roofed Royal Oak is said to have been a pub since it was built in 1540, whilst St Mary's Church dates from the 14th century. The village is also home to the Cerne Abbas Brewery.

THE PUB

The Royal Oak, Cerne Abbas, DT2 7JG.
☎ 01300 341797 www.theroyaloakcerneabbas.co.uk

THE WALK

At the junction of **Long Street** and **Abbey Street**, with the **Royal Oak** pub on your right, head north along **Abbey Street**, soon passing a Tudor period timber-framed building (left) and **St Mary's Church** (right). At

Guide to Dorset Pub Walks

HOW TO GET THERE AND PARKING: Junction of Long Street and Abbey Street in Cerne Abbas; signposted as 'Village Centre & Toilets' off the A352 between Dorchester and Sherborne. There is roadside parking. **Sat Nav:** DT2 7JF.

MAP: OS Explorer 117 Cerne Abbas & Bere Regis. **Grid Ref:** ST665011.

TERRAIN: Short walk with some steep bits, gates and stiles, can be muddy, country lanes.

the end of the road, with **Abbey House** ahead, bear slightly right and turn right through the large gate into the churchyard; before that, keep ahead through the small metal gate to visit the Abbey ruins (entry charge) and then retrace steps. Having entered the churchyard the surfaced path splits, take the left-hand fork and leave through a gate in the wall; to visit **St Augustine's Well** (a sacred natural spring) take the right-hand fork alongside the wall, then retrace your steps and turn right.

2 Once outside the churchyard the path splits. Turn right, keeping the wall on the right, soon passing a large tree; the earthworks over to the right is where the abbey church once stood. Go through a small gate, keep ahead along the left-hand edge and go through a gate in the far left corner. Turn left for a few metres, then turn right. Continue uphill, stopping to admire the views on the way. At the top, go through a gate and keep ahead beside the fence on the left for 175m.

3 Turn left through a gate and head across the field to a four-way junction beside the trees. Turn left across the field (signposted '**Cerne Abbas**') to a stile; you may have to follow the right-hand field edge. Having crossed the stile follow the path south-westwards downhill. Keep to the main path, later contouring round the hill, with trees down to the right. Continue alongside the fence on the left (the giant is hidden up to the left). At the end of the fence keep ahead and then turn right down some steps. Go straight ahead through a gate and follow the path to a track at some farm buildings.

4 Turn left, then right at the junction, soon crossing **Kettle Bridge**; the path to the left just after the bridge is the onward route, before that keep ahead along **Kettle Bridge Lane** to a T-junction. Turn right and then fork right to the **Cerne Giant Viewpoint** (information boards and car park). Retrace your steps and just before Kettle Bridge turn right. Follow the path southwards, keeping the stream on the left and ignoring side paths. Later, pass **Mill House** and continue along the track past buildings and then along **Mill Lane** to a T-junction. Turn left along **Duck Street** to a junction with **The New Inn** opposite and turn left along **Long Street** back to the start.

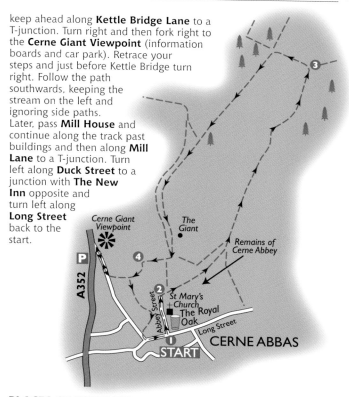

PLACES OF INTEREST NEARBY

Minterne Gardens (DT2 7AU) in Minterne Magna has been described as "a corner of paradise". Here you can wander through the woodland garden with its collection of rhododendrons and azaleas and, although the house is private, there is a nice café on the terrace overlooking the lake.

10 Sutton Poyntz

4 miles / 6.3km

WALK HIGHLIGHTS

Sutton Poyntz, hidden amongst the rolling chalk downs, is home to The Springhead pub overlooking the picturesque River Jordan with its ducks and shady willow trees; the river was used to provide water for Sutton Mill. After a stiff climb the walk follows the South Dorset Ridgeway offering some great views over Weymouth and Portland. On the steep southern slope is the equestrian carving of King George III – a regular visitor to Weymouth; the figure was cut in 1808 and is best viewed from the return route.

THE PUB

The Springhead, Sutton Poyntz, DT3 6LW.
☎ 01305 832117 www.thespringhead.co.uk

THE WALK

1 Walk back along **Plaisters Lane** to the junction and turn sharp left along **Sutton Road**, passing the former **Sutton Mill**. Continue alongside the stream to pass **The Springhead** pub (right) and at the next junction turn left along **Mission Hall Lane** for 10m. Then turn right along the

HOW TO GET THERE AND PARKING: Plaisters Lane in Sutton Poyntz; the village is signposted off the A353 on the eastern edge of Weymouth. Limited roadside parking along Plaisters Lane. **Sat Nav:** DT3 6LQ.

MAP: OS Explorer OL15 Purbeck & South Dorset. **Grid Ref:** SY705836.

TERRAIN: Some steep bits, gates and stiles, can be muddy, and village walking.

track between houses. Go through a gate and follow the track, passing the **Wessex Water station**. Keep ahead past the **Millennium Oak Walk memorial stone** and go over the stile at the end.

Turn left following the hedge on your left up to a junction beside a seat and the **Millennium Beacon**. Keep ahead up the grassy track; stop and admire the views on the way, in the foreground are the earthworks of Charlbury Iron Age hillfort with Weymouth and Portland beyond. At the top go through the small gate, fork right to the top of the field and turn right, now following the hedge on your left over **West Hill**.

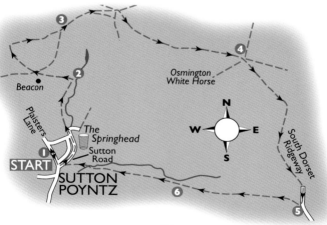

3 Go through the small gate at the corner, continue alongside the hedge through the field and leave through a gate. Here the route splits, fork left, passing just right of a tumulus (Bronze Age burial mound) to a small and large gate. Go through the small gate and follow the enclosed route slightly uphill. Go through a small gate and keep ahead alongside the field edge to the corner.

4 Go through the gate and fork right down the track signed '**South Dorset Ridgeway Osmington ¾**', with views ahead. At the bottom of the slope bear right and continue along the hedge-lined track, later following it as it curves left. The track becomes tarred at the houses. Keep ahead for 150m and then turn right on a track just before the old water pump on the right.

5 Follow the hedge-lined track. Go through a large gate and keep ahead for 10m to cross a stile beside another large gate. Keep ahead along the wide grassy strip between fences; soon there is a view of the Osmington White Horse on the hillside to the right. Cross a stile beside a gate, keep ahead over the crossing track and cross another stile at a gate. Follow the left-hand field edge to the far corner.

6 Cross the stile, pass an old wall and keep ahead through the field to a gate on the far side. Keep ahead through the next field, cross over a track and go through the large gate. Keep to the path as it curves right and then left through a small gate. Continue towards the houses, go through a metal kissing gate and follow the enclosed path between houses to join **Sutton Lane**; to the right is **The Springhead** pub. To return to the start, turn left and then sharp right at the junction back into **Plaisters Lane**.

PLACES OF INTEREST NEARBY

Head to Weymouth for the **Victorian Nothe Fort** (DT4 8UF) and **Henry VIII's Sandsfoot Castle** (DT4 8QE). Or visit Portland, highlights include the **Portland Bill Lighthouse** (DT5 2JT) and **Pulpit Rock**; **Tout Quarry Sculpture Park and nature reserve** (DT5 2LN); and Henry VIII's 16th-century **Portland Castle** (DT5 1AZ).

11 Plush

4½ miles / 7.2km

WALK HIGHLIGHTS

The village of Plush, hidden amongst the rolling chalk downs just east of the main Piddle Valley, is home to The Brace of Pheasants. This picturesque white-washed and thatch-roofed pub, located in a former blacksmith's building, has a very unusual sign – a brace of stuffed pheasants in a glass case. This fairly hilly walk, which has some great views on a clear day, follows parts of two long-distance routes: the Hardy Way and the Wessex Ridgeway.

THE PUB

The Brace of Pheasants, Plush, DT2 7RQ.
☎ 01300 348357 www.braceofpheasants.co.uk.

THE WALK

From the lay-by, with the Victorian **Church of St John the Baptist** behind you, turn right down the road towards the village and follow the road as it curves right to a junction at the **Brace of Pheasants**

Guide to Dorset Pub Walks

HOW TO GET THERE AND PARKING: The Church of St John the Baptist
in Plush; exit the A35 at Puddletown and follow the B3143 through
Piddlehinton to Piddletrenthide and then follow signed minor road to
Plush; park in the small lay-by beside the church. **Sat Nav:** DT2 7RJ.

MAP: OS Explorer 117 Cerne Abbas & Bere Regis. **Grid Ref:** ST718022.

TERRAIN: Hilly with some steep bits, gates and stiles, can be muddy,
lane walking.

pub. Turn left along the road for 75m, then turn right on a track signed
'**Church Hill 1**'. Go through the gate and follow the track steeply uphill.

2 At the top of the rise go through a gate and keep ahead along the
grassy track for 100m to a Y-junction beside a small stone pillar on
Watcombe Plain. Take the left-hand fork towards a hedge and then
continue north, keeping the hedge on your left (this area is open
access land). Pass through a hedge gap and keep ahead to a hedge
and stile. Do not cross the stile but turn right, now following the
Wessex Ridgeway over **Church Hill**, keeping the hedge on your left
for 400m.

3 Start bearing slightly right, away from the hedge, passing just left of
a small rectangular enclosure (earth bank and ditch) to reach the far
field corner. Go through the gate and continue along the track with
Watcombe Wood on your right. At a junction keep left (straight on)
and go through a gate into the field. Continue over **Ball Hill** following
the left-hand hedge. Go through a gate and follow the track downhill,
passing through another gate on the way. At the bottom, go through
a third gate and continue to a lane at **Folly**, passing a house on
your right.

4 Cross straight over and follow a hedge-lined track (signed for '**Dorset
Gap**') up to a Y-junction. Fork right and shortly cross a stile beside a
gate. Follow the sunken way uphill. Near the top go through a gate and
continue in the same direction to a four-way junction on **Lyscombe
Hill**. Turn right, staying in the field and following the left-hand edge,
later passing a trig point which is on the left beyond the fence.

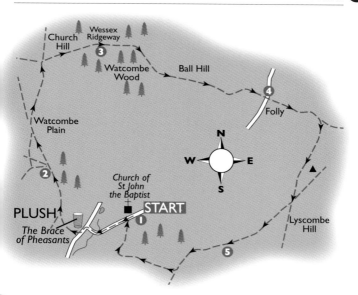

Keep ahead (fence on left), go through a gate and keep left (straight on) still following the fence and go through a small gate at the corner. Continue across the field, aiming for the trees and then continue, keeping the trees on your left. At the corner of the wood turn right across the field, passing to the right of a circular concrete tank. Pass a stile in the hedge and head down to the fence, with views of the village ahead. Go over the stile and follow the route downhill as it quickly curves right. Go through a gate at the bottom and turn right, back to the lay-by beside the church on the left.

PLACES OF INTEREST NEARBY

Visit **Athelhampton House and Garden** (DT2 7LG; www.athelhampton. com) one of England's finest Tudor manor houses, dating from 1485, and explore the beautiful gardens.

12 Sturminster Newton

5¼ miles / 8.3km

WALK HIGHLIGHTS

Sturminster Newton, built at a historic fording point on the River Stour, was home to one of the largest cattle markets in the UK until it closed in 1997. The novelist Thomas Hardy lived here for a while, and the town appears as 'Stourcastle' in his novel *Tess of the d'Urbervilles*. Visit the museum to learn more and then pop across to the thatch-roofed White Hart Alehouse that dates from 1708. Upstream is Hinton St Mary, home to St Peter's Church and a number of picture-postcard thatched cottages.

THE PUB

White Hart Alehouse, Sturminster Newton, DT10 1AN.
☎ 01258 472558 www.whitehartalehouse.co.uk

THE WALK

1 Exit the car park to the right of the toilets and cross over the road and follow **Station Road** (pedestrian zone); just to the right is the **Somerset & Dorset Joint Railway garden**, the railway operated from 1863 until 1966. Turn left along the main road (B3092) and then keep right, crossing via the zebra crossing; to the left is the **Swan Inn**. Follow

HOW TO GET THERE AND PARKING: Station Road car park; turn north off A357 at Sturminster Newton and follow B3092 (signposted 'Town Centre') for ½ mile to a junction (traffic lights), turn right on Old Market Hill (B3091 – towards Shaftesbury) and right along Station Road following signs for parking. **Sat Nav:** DT10 1BN.

MAP: OS Explorer 129 Yeovil & Sherborne. **Grid Ref:** ST787142.

TERRAIN: Some short climbs, gates and stiles, can be muddy especially by the river, road crossings and lane walking.

the B3092 past the old market cross and museum (left) and the **White Hart Alehouse** (right). Turn right along **Ricketts Lane**, pass the car park and follow the path along the right-hand edge of the recreation ground to a path junction in the corner (left goes to **Sturminster Mill**).

Turn right down to a cross-junction and go straight on, soon passing the old railway bridge. Continue through the trees to a kissing gate, then fork right, soon following the top edge of the field. Keep ahead through a gateway into the next field where the path splits. Fork left down to a footbridge (the right-hand fork is the return route). Continue through two fields, separated by a footbridge and kissing gates in some trees, keeping the river on your left.

Go through two small gates and cross a footbridge. Keep ahead through two fields, still following the river. At the field corner follow the path through **Joyce's Coppice**, later bearing right up some steps to a lane and turn right; 100m to the left are the ruins of **Cutt Mill** beside the river. Go up the lane for 30m and turn right (bridleway 'Wood Lane ¾') through Joyce's Coppice. Follow the bridleway into the field and immediately turn left following the left-hand edge to the corner. Turn right for a short way and go left over two stiles in the hedge. Head diagonally right across the field to the corner. Cross a stile beside the large gate and follow the track past buildings as it swings left.

Cross the road (B3092) and follow the lane opposite to a junction and turn right to a T-junction. Turn right to a junction on the left beside the **Village Millennium Garden** (right) and the **White Horse Inn**;

Guide to Dorset Pub Walks

along the lane to the left is **St Peter's Church**. Continue downhill, cross the road (B3092) and follow the lane opposite. At the right-hand bend turn left along the track signed '**Sturminster Newton 1¼ and Sturminster Mill 2¾**'. Keep ahead as the track enters a field with **Twinwood Coppice** on the left and continue to the field corner.

5 Go through the trees, cross a footbridge and through a kissing gate. Continue through the field up to the gate passed earlier. Fork left, soon following the left-hand field edge. Retrace your steps past the kissing gate and through the trees, passing the old railway bridge again to the four-way junction. Turn left uphill, go through a kissing gate and follow the lane. Cross over the B3092 and follow **Station Road** back to the car park.

PLACES OF INTEREST NEARBY

Visit picturesque **Sturminster Mill** on the River Stour (DT10 2DQ; www.sturminsternewton-museum.co.uk/mill) or nearby **Fiddleford Manor** which dates from the 14th century (DT10 2BX; www.english-heritage.org.uk/visit/places/fiddleford-manor).

13 **Milton Abbas**

4½ miles / 7.2km

WALK HIGHLIGHTS

Take a wander through Milton Abbas with its 'picture-postcard' thatched cottages founded by Joseph Damer, Lord Milton and Earl of Dorchester in 1780, shortly after he acquired Milton Abbey. The abbey was originally founded by King Athelstan, grandson of Alfred the Great, in AD 934. Pop inside the stunning building to admire the vaulted ceiling and striking white marble tomb commemorating Damer's wife. The walk also meanders through woods to the north of the village, passing St Catherine's Chapel from where there is a great view of the abbey.

THE PUB

The Hambro Arms, Milton Abbas, DT11 0BP.
☎ 01258 880233 www.hambroarms.com.

THE WALK

Stand facing the **Hambro Arms** and turn right down **The Street** lined with thatched cottages to a junction at the bottom. Turn right, signposted to **Milton Abbey**, using the pavement on the left. Just before the thatched cottage, fork left along the enclosed path. On

41

Guide to Dorset Pub Walks

HOW TO GET THERE AND PARKING: The Hambro Arms; from the A354 at Winterborne Whitechurch follow a minor road signposted to Milton Abbas and turn left down The Street, roadside parking near the pub. **Sat Nav:** DT11 0BP.

MAP: OS Explorer 117 Cerne Abbas & Bere Regis. **Grid Ref:** ST808019.

TERRAIN: Some ups and downs, gates, no stiles, can be muddy, road walking.

reaching the school grounds keep ahead along the track (right of way) to Milton Abbey. Having admired the abbey, retrace your steps back to the thatched cottage beside the road and turn left, following the minor road with care for 450m to a track junction on the right.

2 Turn sharp right up the track to a four-way junction; on the right is **Steeptonbill Farm shop and café**. Turn sharp left, signed '**St Catherine's Chapel ¼**' and continue to the small chapel with its view of the abbey. Keep ahead past the chapel, keeping right at a junction heading uphill. Turn left at the next junction along the wide track, later ignoring two paths to the left. Pass a vehicle barrier to join a gravel drive and bear left to a cross junction (on the right is a large set of gateposts, ornamental metal gates and gatehouses). Keep ahead to a junction just after passing another vehicle barrier.

3 Turn left on a narrow track through the trees. Keep ahead along the track heading downhill and later curving right. Continue along the track which later heads up to a track junction. Turn left and soon bear right past a vehicle barrier to a small parking area next to a minor road. Turn hard right and follow the signed bridleway through some trees. Continue along the right-hand field edge with trees beyond. Later there is a wooden fence on the left, where this turns left, keep left, following the fence line to a gravel drive (to the right is a private garden).

4 Turn right, passing a house entrance on the right, and just before the large gates seen earlier in the walk, turn left on a signed bridleway through the trees. Follow the right-hand field edge to the far right lower corner, crossing a track on the way. Go through the gap and bear left on a bridleway over open ground towards some houses. Turn right down the road to a T-junction and cross diagonally right. Follow the tarred path through the small park and then turn left down the road, keeping ahead at the cross-junction to a T-junction. Turn left and then right into a cul-de-sac. Bear right to a gravel drive and fork left along the narrow bridleway, going left and right down through the trees. Exit onto the road (**The Street**) and turn right along the pavement back to the start.

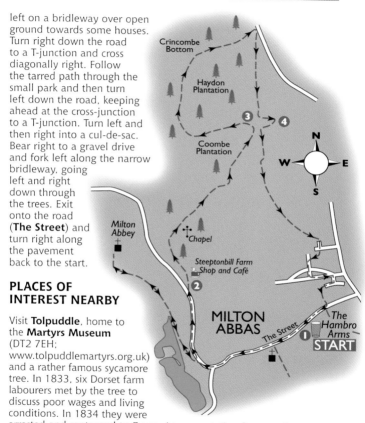

PLACES OF INTEREST NEARBY

Visit **Tolpuddle**, home to the **Martyrs Museum** (DT2 7EH; www.tolpuddlemartyrs.org.uk) and a rather famous sycamore tree. In 1833, six Dorset farm labourers met by the tree to discuss poor wages and living conditions. In 1834 they were arrested and sentenced to 7 years' transportation for swearing a secret oath and forming a Trade Union. However, countrywide mass protests eventually led to their full pardoning.

14 Child Okeford

4½ miles / 7.1km or 6 miles / 9.7km

WALK HIGHLIGHTS

A hilly route offering some great views starting from Child Okeford, home to the red-brick Baker Arms pub which dates back to the 1750s and the late 15th-century St Nicholas' Church. High above is Hambledon Hill, a national nature reserve for its classic chalk downland habitat, crowned by the earthworks of an impressive Iron Age hillfort. The longer route also visits Hod Hill which, like its near neighbour, is crowned by an Iron Age hillfort that offers more great views.

THE PUB

The Baker Arms, Child Okeford, DT11 8ED.
☎ 01258 860260 www.bakerarms.co.uk.

THE WALK

1 Stand at the **War Memorial** looking at the **Baker Arms** and go right, then immediately right along the road towards **Irwene Minster**. After 150m turn right (**Manor Barn** entrance) and immediately turn left up some steps. Go through a gate and fork left alongside the left-hand field edge. Leave through a gate, turn right through a gate and follow the tree-shaded path to a gate.

HOW TO GET THERE AND PARKING: Roadside parking in the village; from Sturminster Newton follow the A357 east towards Shillingstone for 2¾ miles and turn left towards Child Okeford. At the T-junction turn left (Manston) along the High Street; limited roadside parking near the village shop. **Sat Nav:** DT11 8ED.

MAP: OS Explorer 118 Shaftesbury & Cranborne Chase.
Grid Ref: ST835128.

TERRAIN: Very hilly with several steep bits, stiles, can be muddy, village lane walking.

② Pass the National Trust sign and follow the path steeply up **Hambledon Hill**; it's quite a climb so stop and admire the view on the way. Continue along the ridge-top path to the far side and follow the track through the earthworks and then a gate. Keep ahead to a four-way bridleway junction beside the trig point.

③ Turn left down the track between open fields, passing a gate to a track junction in front of the wall. Turn right (wall on left) to the corner of the wood on your left. Go left and quickly fork right on a bridleway with trees on your left, following the power line. Keep ahead through two gates to enter a field.

④ **Decision time: for the shorter walk** turn right up the field edge, pass a barn and go through a gate, continue from **Point 6. For the longer walk** keep ahead for 400m, go through gates either side of a lane and follow the left-hand field edge to the corner. Continue through the trees, then a gate and follow the field edge. Join a track and keep ahead as it curves to the right to a gate. Do not go through but turn right and go through a field entrance beside a sign for **Hod Hill**.

⑤ Turn left alongside the fence (left) to a four-way junction. Turn right heading through the earthworks, continue over the hill and then down past more earthworks. Go through a gate, fork half-right downhill and through a gate. Cross the lane and enter a field to the right of a house entrance. Follow the track steeply up the left-hand edge, turn left after a barn and through a gate.

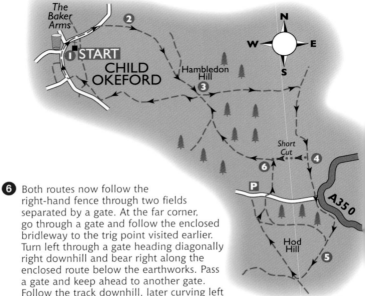

6 Both routes now follow the right-hand fence through two fields separated by a gate. At the far corner, go through a gate and follow the enclosed bridleway to the trig point visited earlier. Turn left through a gate heading diagonally right downhill and bear right along the enclosed route below the earthworks. Pass a gate and keep ahead to another gate. Follow the track downhill, later curving left and continue to the lane. Immediately turn sharp-right over a stile beside the field gate. Keep ahead along the enclosed path, keep left and then turn left through a gate. Follow the gravel drive and turn right along the road back to the **Baker Arms**.

PLACES OF INTEREST NEARBY

Visit **Shaftesbury** for great views over Thomas Hardy's Blackmore Vale and admire the picturesque Gold Hill (SP7 8LY), a steep cobbled street made famous by the "Hovis" advert. Or visit the **Abbey Museum and Garden** (SP7 8JR) to learn about the former abbey.

15 Wareham

4 miles / 6.5km

WALK HIGHLIGHTS

The bustling historic town of Wareham sits between the River Frome and River Piddle as they make their way to Poole Harbour. Looking out across the River Frome is the Old Granary pub with its riverside terrace. The walk follows parts of the earth ramparts that formed the town's Saxon defences against invaders. Inside the Church of St Martin's-on-The-Walls there are some 12th-century frescoes and an effigy of T.E. Lawrence (aka Lawrence of Arabia). The larger Priory Church of Lady St Mary houses a rare, early 12th-century hexagonal lead font decorated with figures of the 12 apostles. The meadows and reed beds are great for wildlife, so don't forget your binoculars.

THE PUB

The Old Granary, Wareham, BH20 4LP.
☎ 01929 552010 www.theoldgranarywareham.co.uk

THE WALK

Exit the car park, cross over the B3070, turn left and then immediately right along **Pound Lane**, passing a former brewery. Follow the lane

47

Guide to Dorset Pub Walks

HOW TO GET THERE AND PARKING: Streche Road car park; from the roundabout at the junction of the A352 and A351 just west of Wareham follow the B3070 signposted for the town centre for ½ mile and turn left into Streche Road (long stay pay and display car park). **Sat Nav:** BH20 4QJ.

MAP: OS Explorer OL15: Purbeck and South Dorset. **Grid Ref:** SY920873.

TERRAIN: Mostly flat, no stiles, can be quite muddy in places (wear appropriate footwear).

as it curves left and turn right along **Tanner's Lane**, then turn left along **Abbot's Quay** with the **River Frome** on the right. Cross the road (B3075) and keep ahead through **The Quay** to the far left corner; over to the right is **The Old Granary** pub. Keep ahead to **Church Green** and bear right to the **Priory Church of Lady St Mary**. Follow **Church Street** (churchyard on right) and then turn right along **Church Lane**

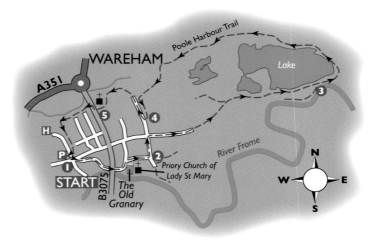

(churchyard on right), following the signs for the **Two Rivers Walk** and **Walls Walk**. Follow the lane as it swings left and right, passing between the churchyards to a T-junction at the end.

❷ Turn left along the lane and keep right at the junction (houses on left) to a staggered crossroads. Turn right along the road (**Bestwell Road**), leave the houses behind and continue along the tarred track (private road – footpath only). Where this turns left to **Swineham**, keep ahead through a gate and follow the path. Go through a gate to a path junction beside a small inlet and boat mooring.

❸ Bear left following the path as it soon swings left. Keep ahead through a kissing gate and continue for ½ mile with trees on the left; this section can be muddy. On reaching a kissing gate (signed '**Wareham ¾**') beside a large gate, turn left through it. Keep ahead along the tree-shaded track and then the tarred lane which soon curves left. Continue for 175m past three houses on the left to a path junction.

❹ Turn right and immediately right again to follow a path along the top of the embankment (remains of the Saxon walls). Keep to the embankment as it swings left and on nearing a house, go straight on along the lane to a junction. Turn left along **St Martin's Lane** (Walls Walk sign) for 50m, then turn right along the path to the **Church of St Martin's-on-The-Walls**.

❺ Bear left to the B3075, turn right across the road and then turn right along the pavement to a junction. Turn left up **Shatters Hill** to a junction with **Mill Lane** (left). Ignore the path to the right but go ahead up the bank to continue along the wall path with a lane on your left. Keep to the top of the embankment as it swings left, cross a minor road and then continue along the bank to a junction with the B3070; the car park entrance is on the right.

PLACES OF INTEREST NEARBY

Head over to **Moreton** to visit **Clouds Hill**, the former home of T. E. Lawrence, aka Lawrence of Arabia (BH20 7NQ; www.nationaltrust. org.uk/clouds-hill) and visit **St Nicholas' Church** (DT2 8RH) to see the beautiful series of engraved glass windows by Sir Laurence Whistler.

16 Worth Matravers

5¼ miles / 8.5km

WALK HIGHLIGHTS

A rollercoaster of a walk with some great views, a lot of steps and the wonderfully-named Square and Compass pub, with its interesting fossil museum and outdoor seating area. The walk follows part of the South West Coast Path past Winspit Quarry before arriving at the atmospheric 13th-century St Aldhelm's Chapel. After a steep descent and climb the next stop is the Royal Marines Commando Memorial, before a fairly level walk back to Worth Matravers.

THE PUB

The Square and Compass, Worth Matravers, BH19 3LF.
☎ 01929 439229 www.squareandcompasspub.co.uk

THE WALK

1 Exit the car park, turn right down the road to a junction and turn left, with the **Square and Compass** pub on your left. Follow the lane for 150m and just before the first house on the right, turn sharp right through a gate beside the National Trust sign for **East Man**. Follow the left-hand boundary to a footpath sign and turn left over the stone stile. Continue down through the field, later down steps and go through a gate at the bottom. Follow the valley towards the sea and bear right along the track.

HOW TO GET THERE AND PARKING: Worth Matravers car park; from Corfe Castle follow the A351 towards Swanage and at the edge of the village turn right on the B3069 towards Langton Matravers. Keep to the B3069 at Kingston to reach a junction after 1 mile and turn right to Worth Matravers; the car park is on the right as you enter the village. **Sat Nav:** BH19 3LE.

MAP: OS Explorer OL15: Purbeck and South Dorset. **Grid Ref:** SY974776.

TERRAIN: Some very steep bits with steps, stiles, can be muddy, village walking.

❷ At the signed path junction turn right; the walk now follows the **South West Coast Path** for 3 miles. Go through a gate, up some steps and through another gate. Turn left following the coastal path with the sea on your left. Go through kissing gates as the path passes a large hole and continue for 500m. Bear right, go through a kissing gate and down steps to a track; to the left is former **Winspit Quarry**, to the right the track heads back to **Worth Matravers**.

❸ Turn right for 20m, then turn left following the coast path up steps and skirting round the top of the quarry (care required). Continue for a mile, later heading uphill and passing the **radar memorial** to reach the lookout station at **St Aldhelm's Head**. Nearby is the **St Aldhelm's Chapel**.

❹ The next stage of the walk involves a lot of steps; anyone not wishing to follow this section should take the signed track past the chapel back to **Worth Matravers** (2 miles). To continue the walk keep ahead along the coast path, descending the steps and then climbing the steps up the other side; take your time and enjoy the views. Continue along the coastal path, cross a stone stile and skirt round the stone wall at the **Royal Marines Commando Memorial**.

❺ Continue along the coast path for 450m to a junction and turn right through a gate. Head across the field, go through a gate beside the car park and cross the lane. Go through another gate and follow the left-hand field boundary straight on. Leave through a gate and bear left past the buildings at **Weston Farm**. Turn right along the lane towards

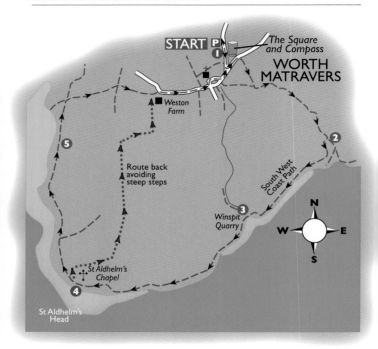

the village. At the junction go left and follow the road round to the right (church on left) and shortly pass the duck pond. Go left at the junction and keep left at the next (Square and Compass on your right) to reach the car park on the left.

PLACES OF INTEREST NEARBY

Visit the picturesque village of **Corfe Castle** home to the stark ruins of **Corfe Castle**, founded by the Normans and partially destroyed during the English Civil War in 1646.

17 Pamphill

3½ miles / 5.6km

WALK HIGHLIGHTS

Take an easy wander along paths and lanes around Pamphill just to the west of Wimborne Minster, which itself is well worth a visit. The hamlet is home to the cosy Vine Inn which was a bakery until 1900, CAMRA states that the "historic pub interior is of national importance", there are also a number of picturesque thatched cottages, St Stephen's Church, and a school built in 1698. The walk also follows parts of the Stour Valley Way and makes a quick visit to a lovely spot on the River Stour.

THE PUB

Vine Inn, Pamphill, BH21 4EE.
☎ 01202 882259 no website

THE WALK

From the car park turn right along the minor road for 100m to a footpath sign and turn left across the grass. Continue through the trees to a field gate and cross the stile. Keep ahead through the field,

Guide to Dorset Pub Walks

HOW TO GET THERE AND PARKING: Pamphill Green car park; follow
the B3082 west from Wimborne Minster for 1½ miles to a crossroads
and follow the signed lane for Pamphill for ¼ mile and turn left,
Pamphill Green car park is on the right. **Sat Nav:** BH21 4ED.

MAP: OS Explorer 118: Shaftesbury & Cranborne Chase.
  Grid Ref: ST990007.

TERRAIN: Gentle ups and downs, stiles, can be muddy, some lane
walking.

cross a stile and descend through the next field. Cross another stile
and continue uphill, keeping left of a thatched cottage. Go over a stile
and turn left along the drive to the road (B3082). Turn right along the
pavement for 300m and turn right through a kissing gate.

2 Follow the enclosed path, cross a footbridge and go through a kissing
gate. Follow the left-hand field edge to a gate on the left and turn right
down to a stile, with a large pylon ahead. Continue through the woods,
cross a footbridge and keep ahead at a junction up some steps to a
large pylon. Turn left to a lane beside a thatched cottage.

3 Turn left down the lane passing the **Vine Inn** (left) and a thatched
cottage (right) to reach a T-junction. Cross straight over and follow the
signed path towards the **River Stour**. Turn right at the path junction,
soon leaving the field over a stile to enter a parking area where the
walk goes right to a lane. To the left is a great picnic spot beside the
River Stour at **Eye Bridge** (there is also a 2-mile signed National Trust
walk from here – see the information board).

4 Turn left along the lane for 50m to a junction then fork right following
the road signposted for **Pamphill School**. Just after the school, turn left
to follow the signed path along the left-hand edge of the playing field to
a path junction. Turn left through the trees for a few metres and continue
along the track to its end. Go through the right-hand gate, head down
through the field to cross a stile at the bottom left corner. Immediately
keep left at the path junction, down a couple of steps and along the
narrow path. Go through a gate and follow the track ahead to a lane.

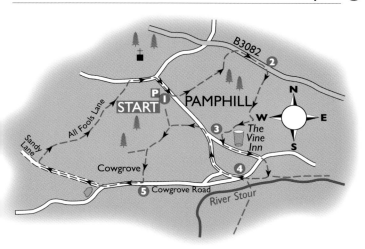

Turn right and at the slight bend (with **Drews Cottage** on the left), fork right along the track between a small pond (left) and **Poplar Farm** (right). Follow the track past **Poplar Farm Cottage**, later passing a large gate beside a red-brick cottage. Just before **Sandy Lane**, turn right up **All Fools Lane** (an ancient tree-shaded route) signed '**Stour Valley Way Pamphill**'. At the top, fork right past a carved seat depicting the **Stour Valley Way** and continue along the lane to a junction. To the left is the early 20th-century **St Stephen's Church**, but to finish the walk turn right back to the car park on the right.

PLACES OF INTEREST NEARBY

The National Trust's **Kingston Lacy**, built to resemble a Venetian Palace, is a short way along the B3082 (BH21 4EA; www.nationaltrust.org.uk/kingston-lacy). Visit the remains of an Iron Age hillfort at **Badbury Rings** (DT11 9JL) or take a wander round historic **Wimborne Minister** with its lovely church (BH21 1EB).

18 Gussage All Saints

5 miles / 7.9km

WALK HIGHLIGHTS

Gussage All Saints, one of three Gussage villages, the others being Gussage St Andrew and Gussage St Michael, is home to the Drovers Inn. The pub closed in late 2014, however, the community pulled together and fought the closure with great success as the pub was re-opened in 2016 as a community-owned venture. The village church, All Saints, mostly dates from the 14th and 15th centuries, though the font is Norman, it's also said that the organ came from Westminster Abbey. Just to the west of the village is Ackling Dyke, which formed part of the main Roman Road from London to Exeter.

THE PUB

The Drovers Inn, Gussage All Saints, BH21 5ET.
☎ 01258 840550 www.thedroversinn.info

THE WALK

1 Stand at the little village green and **War Memorial** in Gussage All Saints looking towards the church and turn left down the lane, cross the

HOW TO GET THERE AND PARKING: Gussage All Saints church; from Blandford Forum follow the A354 for 5½ miles, turn right along a minor road towards Horton, then left at the crossroads and continue through Gussage St Michael to Gussage All Saints, roadside parking near the small village green and War Memorial at the western end of the village. **Sat Nav:** BH21 5ET.

MAP: OS Explorer 118: Shaftesbury & Cranborne Chase.
Grid Ref: ST998107.

TERRAIN: Gentle ups and downs, no gates or stiles, can be muddy, some lane walking.

bridge over the stream and turn right at the junction towards **Gussage St Michael**. Follow the minor road for 500m passing a thatched cottage on your right and **Manor Farm** on your left to a track on the right beside a lay-by, information board and picnic table.

2 Turn right, crossing a brick bridge and passing a vehicle barrier and continue along the hedge-lined track (**James Cross Lane**) – the walk is now following the course of **Ackling Dyke**, a former Roman Road for 1¾ miles. Keep ahead past a large barn, still rising gently. Ignore a bridleway on the right and continue with a fenced meadow on the right. Then continue through the wood to a cross junction at **Harley Gap**.

3 Turn right, leaving Ackling Dyke and head through the trees for 50m to a signed junction. Turn right and follow the track through the trees soon swinging to the left and following the edge of the wood, with **Harley Wood** on your right and a field to the left. At the track junction keep right and continue with the wood on your right and fields on the left; later ignore a track to the right. Keep ahead at two track junctions (bridleway) 50m apart.

Guide to Dorset Pub Walks

4 Continue along the track (**Harley Lane**), pass a vehicle barrier and just after the first house on the right, turn left beside a gate (footpath sign) and follow the track past **College Farm**. Keep to the right-hand track (straight on) past the house and continue along the field edge to a junction. Turn right to a lane and turn right again beside **The Drovers Inn** which is on your right and follow the lane back to the village green, with **All Saints Church** ahead.

PLACES OF INTEREST NEARBY

Visit the atmospheric ruins of the **Norman church at Knowlton** (BH21 5AE), situated within an ancient Neolithic henge earthwork. Or head to the market town of **Blandford Forum** on the River Stour, said to be the most complete small Georgian town in England. Here you can take a tour of the **Hall and Woodhouse Brewery** (DT11 9LS; www.hall-woodhouse.co.uk).

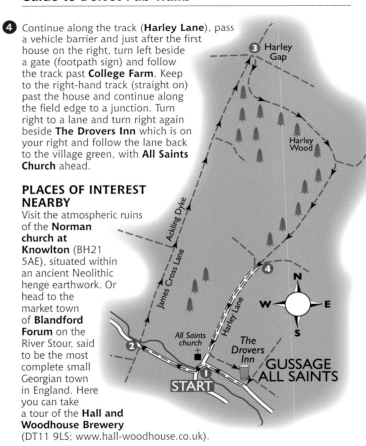

19 Studland & Old Harry

5¾ miles / 9.2km

WALK HIGHLIGHTS

Head to the Isle of Purbeck for a hilly figure-of-eight walk from the outskirts of Swanage; a quick look at the map will show that the walk can easily be shortened or started from Studland if required. After heading over Ballard Down we arrive at the picturesque little village of Studland, home to the Bankes Arms Inn with its large beer garden. Form here it's an easy walk out to the wonderful Old Harry Rocks, one of Dorset's most famous landmarks. After admiring the views we soon head west along the top of Ballard Down to reach The Obelisk, with more great views on the way.

THE PUB

The Bankes Arms Inn, Studland, BH19 3AU.
☎ 01929 450225 www.bankesarms.com

Guide to Dorset Pub Walks

HOW TO GET THERE AND PARKING: Ulwell Road lay-by; from Studland follow the B3351 for ¾ mile, then fork left towards Swanage for 1 mile to Ulwell, park in the second large lay-by on the left beside the stone sign for Swanage. **Sat Nav:** BH19 3DG.

MAP: OS Explorer OL15: Purbeck and South Dorset. **Grid Ref:** SZ021809.

TERRAIN: Hilly walk with several steep bits and a descent with steps, no stiles, can be muddy, village lanes.

THE WALK

1 With your back to the road go through the kissing gate beside the large gate. Follow the path along the left edge for 60m to a four-way junction. Turn right and follow the path eastwards for ½ mile to a four-way junction. Fork left up the stony bridleway to another four-way junction at the top, beside a stone seat.

2 Continue in the same direction downhill, firstly on a grassy path that soon becomes a stony track. Go through a small gate beside the large gate and bear right following the tarred track downhill. At **Manor Farm**, where there is a tearoom, bear right to join a road with a large carved stone cross opposite. Keep right down the road to the left-hand bend with the toilets opposite, the onwards route takes the track straight on (toilets on left). But before that, detour left along the road for 80m to **The Bankes Arms Inn**; retrace your steps and turn left just after the toilets.

3 Follow the **South West Coast Path** along the track and where the track goes left (private), continue along the narrower route, ignoring all side paths to reach the cliffs at **Handfast Point** overlooking the **Old Harry Rocks**. After enjoying the wonderful views turn right following the coast path up along the edge of the cliffs with the sea on your left; on the way, there is a good view of **The Pinnacles** (sea stacks eroded from the chalk cliffs). Ignore a gate on the right and continue, keeping the fence on your right as it curves right at **Ballard Point**. Continue uphill and at the top go through the small gate at the fence corner. Bear half-right to the trig point.

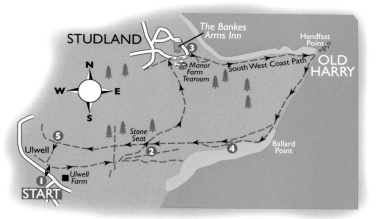

4 Continue westwards along the top of **Ballard Down** for slightly over ½ mile to arrive at the junction beside the stone seat passed earlier (Point 2; anyone wanting to avoid the steep steps at the end of the walk can retrace the outward route from here back to the start). To continue with the walk keep ahead uphill with views of **Swanage** to the left and **Poole Harbour**, Europe's largest natural harbour, to the right. Pass over the summit and head down to **The Obelisk** (built in 1883 to mark the opening of a new drinking water supply for Swanage).

5 Turn left through the gate and follow the path signed 'Ulwell ¼' downhill, soon heading down the rather steep flight of stone steps. On reaching the four-way junction passed at the start of the walk, keep ahead and shortly go through the kissing gate back to the parking area.

PLACES OF INTEREST NEARBY

Visit **Durlston Country Park and National Nature Reserve**, home to nature trails and a Victorian 'castle' (BH19 2JL; www.durlston.co.uk). Take a trip on the **Swanage Railway** (BH19 1HB; www.swanagerailway.co.uk) or visit **RSPB Arne** (BH20 5BJ) for nature trails and birdwatching.

20 Cranborne

4½ miles / 7.1km

WALK HIGHLIGHTS

Picturesque Cranborne lies along the River Crane in the far north-east corner of Dorset on the edge of Cranborne Chase, a former Royal hunting ground. Cranborne Manor, originally a hunting lodge for King John, dates from the 13th century whilst along Castle Street is Cranborne Lodge (now a hotel and restaurant known as 10 Castle Street) that was built for Henry VIII. The Church of St Mary and St Bartholomew was once part of Cranborne Priory. The village is also home to the 16th-century Fleur de Lys Inn, used by Thomas Hardy in his novel, *Tess of the d'Urbervilles* in which Cranborne became 'Chaseborough'; the poet Rupert Brooke also wrote a poem about the inn after getting lost trying to reach it.

THE PUB

The Fleur de Lys Inn, Cranborne, BH21 5PP.
☎ 01725 551249 www.thefleurdelysinn.co.uk

THE WALK

❶ From **The Square**, with the village shop and post office on your left, head along the pavement passing the **Sheaf of Arrows** pub (left) and

HOW TO GET THERE AND PARKING: The Square in Cranborne; follow the B3081 for 4 miles heading south-east from the A354 at Handley Cross or follow the B3078 west from the A338 at Fordingbridge for 7 miles; on-street parking in The Square or there is a car park beside the primary school in Water Street. **Sat Nav:** BH21 5PR.

MAP: OS Explorer 118: Shaftesbury & Cranborne Chase and OS Explorer OL22: New Forest. **Grid Ref:** SU055133.

TERRAIN: Gentle ups and downs, no stiles, can be muddy, some lane walking.

La Fosse restaurant (right). Keep right past the little square following the **High Street** as it swings right and then turn left along the track (bridleway sign) between house numbers 15 and 17. Go through the gate and keep ahead crossing an avenue of trees; look left for a glimpse of **Cranborne Manor**. Keep ahead, go through a gate and follow the track past a house (left) to join a surfaced track.

❷ Keep right past buildings including the award-winning **Book and Bucket Cheese Company** and follow the surfaced track for ¾ mile to buildings at **Cranborne Farm**. Turn right up the track (**Jubilee Trail** signs) for slightly over ½ mile to a cross-junction with the **Hardy Way** just after the brow of the hill at **Jack's Hedge Corner**. Keep ahead past the gate and follow the right-hand field edge downhill. Turn right along the track passing a large barn (left), then fork right at the junction. Continue along the level track for 600m to a road junction.

❸ Cross straight over, passing the thatched cottage (right) and follow the minor road for 400m to a Y-junction. Keep right, following the road for a further 100m to a gate on your right. Turn right past the gate, following the footpath signed for '**Burwood Pit ½**'. Continue up through the trees, then downhill, ignoring a track to the right, then one to the left and pass a timber yard to a minor road.

❹ Turn right along the road for 40m and then turn left through a hedge gap beside a footpath sign. Follow the right-hand field edge down to a T-junction and turn right (the path to the left leads to **Holwell Farm**

and the **Sixpenny Brewery**; www.sixpennybrewery.co.uk). After 80m go left down a narrow path to an estate road (**Friday's Heron**). Turn right for 50m and then fork left to a stream.

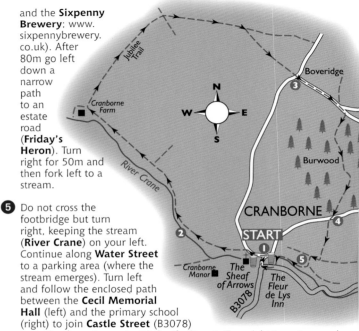

5 Do not cross the footbridge but turn right, keeping the stream (**River Crane**) on your left. Continue along **Water Street** to a parking area (where the stream emerges). Turn left and follow the enclosed path between the **Cecil Memorial Hall** (left) and the primary school (right) to join **Castle Street** (B3078) opposite the entrance to **10 Castle Street**. Turn right to a staggered junction beside **The Fleur De Lys Inn**. **Church Street** opposite leads to the **Church of St Mary and St Bartholomew**. Turn right along **Wimborne Street**, then left at the junction back to **The Square**.

PLACES OF INTEREST NEARBY

Take a stroll around the **Manor Garden** that surrounds **Cranborne Manor** (BH21 5PY; www.cranborne.co.uk) or head over to the **Dorset Heavy Horse Farm Park** near **Verwood** (BH21 5RJ; www.dorset-heavy-horse-centre.co.uk).